Happy Birthday Christopher
September 30, 1997
Love, Grandpa & Grandma Ji

P9-EDV-389

Observing the Sky

Carole Stott

Troll Associates

Library of Congress Cataloging-in-Publication Data

Stott, Carole.
    Observing the sky / by Carole Stott.
      p.   cm.—(Exploring the universe)
    Summary: Presents tips on how to view stars, planets, eclipses,
comets, and meteors, and discusses how astronomers use telescopes to
study the sky.
    ISBN 0-8167-2132-7 (lib. bdg.)   ISBN 0-8167-2133-5 (pbk.)
    1. Astronomy—Observers' manuals—Juvenile literature.
[1. Astronomy—Observers' manuals.] I. Title. II. Series:
Exploring the universe.
QB64.S76 1991
520—dc20   90-11018

Published by Troll Associates, Mahwah, New Jersey 07430

Copyright © 1991 Eagle Books Limited

All rights reserved. No part of this book may be reproduced or
utilized in any form or by any means, electronic or mechanical,
including photocopying, recording or by any storage and retrieval
system, without permission in writing from the Publisher.

Edited by Neil Morris
Design by Sally Boothroyd
Picture research by Carole Stott and Karen Gunnell

Printed in the U.S.A.

10 9 8 7 6 5 4 3 2 1

Illustrations:
Rhoda & Robert Burns/Drawing Attention pp 11, 12, 28
Paul Doherty cover, pp 17, 21
Julie Douglas p 7
William Morris p 27
Julia Osorno p 9

Picture credits:
European Southern Observatory pp 29 (bottom), 31 (top)
Federation of Astronomical Societies pp 9, 10, 23 (bottom);
   (Ruth Bradford-Harris) 4; (David Early) 14; (John
   Laidlaw) 13; (Kim Lindley) 22; (Michael Pace) 20;
   (Robin Scagell) 5, 8; (David Strange) 15, 16
Akira Fujii pp 1, 2-3, 18, 21, 23 (top), 25, 27, 31 (bottom)
David Hughes p 24
Robert McNaught p 19
NASA pp 7, 17, 29 (top), 30
National Optical Astronomy Observatories back
   cover
Robin Scagell p 26
Survival Anglia pp 6-7

Front cover: the southern-sky Milky Way.
Title page: the Moon.
Pages 2-3: the constellation of Sagittarius.

Contents

The sky above

Observing the sky above gives each of us the chance to explore space. From Earth, we can look up and see hundreds of thousands of stars. Many are stars like our Sun. Some are older, others younger. We can even see stars that are grouped together into galaxies millions and millions of miles away. Closer to us are planets like our Earth. Some planets are enormous balls of rock, and there are others made of gas. The Moon is so close, we can see its mountains and valleys. We can see all of this in the dark night sky.

In the daytime, the sky is lit up by the Sun. There are other stars in the sky during the day, too, but it is impossible to see them because the Sun's light is so strong. The Sun is the most important star for Earth. It gives us light and heat. Without the Sun, there would be no life on Earth, no plants, no animals, and no people.

▲ The Moon is a marvelous object for any young astronomer to study and enjoy. It is one of the most beautiful and easily seen objects in the night sky.

◄ There are thousands of pinpoints of light in the night sky. At first it seems an impossible task to tell them apart, but you can soon become familiar with them. You'll also discover that they are not all single stars. They may be a pair, a cluster, or even a whole galaxy of stars.

Each day the Sun rises in the east. We see it getting higher and higher in the sky until noon, then lower and lower until it disappears behind the Earth in the west. Thousands of years ago, some people thought the Sun was a god traveling across the sky in a fiery chariot. Now we know that the Sun is a star, and it is simply the Earth spinning around once a day that makes the Sun appear to move in this way.

Daytime star

Not only does the Sun give us our day, it also sets the pattern of our year. The Earth takes a year (or, to be precise, 365¼ days) to travel around the Sun. As the year progresses, the length of time the Sun is in the sky each day changes. When the Sun rises early in the morning and sets late at night, it is summer. At midsummer, the Sun is at its highest and we feel more of its heat. In winter, the days are shorter and colder because the Sun is not in the sky for as long.

The Sun is good for us, but only because it is about 93 million miles away. It is an enormous ball of gas 109 times bigger than the Earth. Its center is extremely hot: 27,000,000°F.

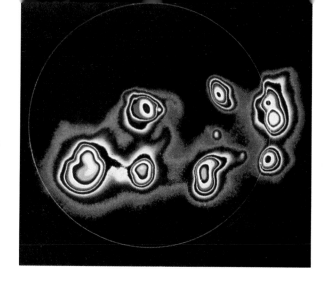

This is where it produces its heat and light. If we were much closer to the Sun, the Earth would be far too hot for us to survive.

The Sun is of great interest to astronomers because it is the closest star to Earth and they can study it in great detail. They use specially designed equipment, as it is dangerous to look straight at the Sun: Its light is so strong it can damage your eyes.

▲ This x-ray photograph shows areas of violent activity within and on the surface of the Sun.

◄ Our star, the Sun, is close enough to us to look different from other stars which appear to be pinpoints of light in the night sky. In this dramatic view of the setting Sun, the camera reveals its round shape to us. We have discovered more of the Sun's secrets by using other equipment on Earth and in space.

▶ You should never look directly at the Sun. Don't be tempted to take even a quick glance at it. Its light is extremely powerful, and it can damage your eyes. Instead, you can use binoculars to collect the sunlight and project it onto a piece of white cardboard or paper. You can then safely look at this projected image of the Sun.

The night sky

Each of the stars that shines in the sky is like our Sun – a very hot, enormous ball of gas. Each one is also very bright, but because they are so far away from us, they look like pinpoints of light. On a clear, dark night, you can see hundreds of stars, or thousands if you use binoculars. There are so many, it is difficult to tell them apart.

Two thousand years ago, people looking at the night sky had the same problem. So they joined the pinpoints of light together to make pictures, just as we connect the dots in puzzle books. It was easy to remember the pictures and recognize the stars. They often named the pictures after animals and people from their folk stories. We still use many of their pictures, called constellations, today. Their bull, bear, and lion are easy to recognize, but

others are less familiar.

Do you know what a scorpion is? Have you heard of Orion? The scorpion, a small creature with crablike claws and a poisonous tail, stung the giant hunter Orion and stopped him from killing the Earth's animals.

Astronomers divide the sky into 88 areas, or constellations. Each of the 88 areas is named after a "picture" constellation in that area. They are each known by the Latin name for the picture their stars make. Ursa Major is the Great Bear; Leo, the Lion; Taurus, the Bull; and Scorpius, the Scorpion.

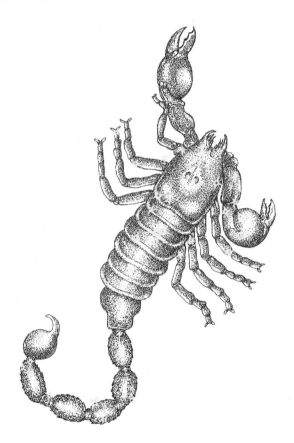

▲ This drawing of a scorpion shows how the constellation of Scorpius (shown in the photograph on the right) got its name.

◄ By grouping the stars into constellations, you will come to know the night sky. Imagine the three stars in the center of this picture as a belt around a man's waist. Below it two stars mark his knees, above it two mark his shoulders. You have just learned the constellation of Orion.

Stargazing

It is a great feeling to look up at the night sky and recognize some of the constellations. It is your first step on the pathway to becoming an astronomer. From a backyard, or better yet, from the darker countryside, you'll see plenty of constellations, but not all 88.

From different parts of the Earth you get a different view of space. If you are in Europe, the United States, Canada, or anywhere else in the Northern Hemisphere (the northern half of the Earth), you will see one set of constellations. If you are in the Southern Hemisphere (in Australia for example) you will see others.

Let's start by taking a look at the constellations of the northern sky. There are five constellations that are always visible. They are the two bears (Ursa Major and Ursa Minor), Draco (the Dragon), and a queen and king called Cassiopeia and Cepheus.

Seven bright stars in the Great Bear (Ursa Major) are among the easiest stars to identify. They are often called the Big Dipper, but many people remember them because they look like a saucepan. These five constellations and all the other northern-sky constellations appear to move around one bright star called Polaris. This star, often called the North Star, is at the tip of the Little Bear's tail.

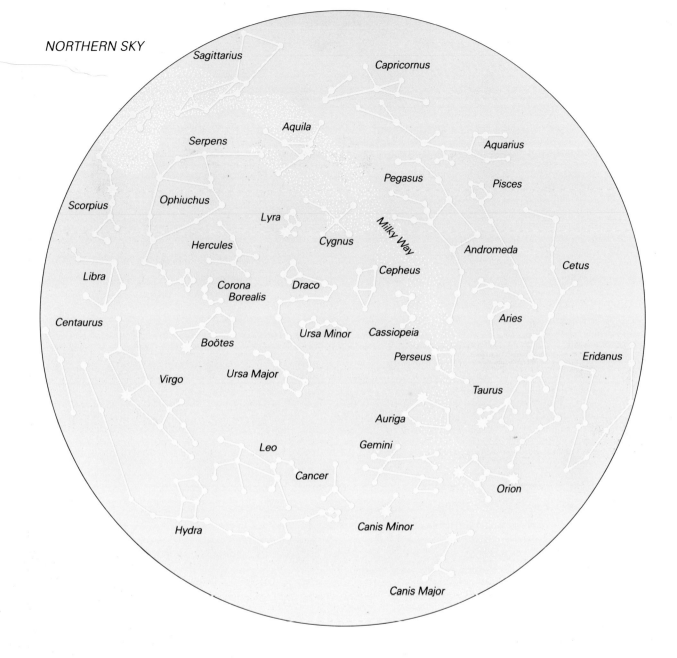

NORTHERN SKY

Sagittarius
Capricornus
Aquila
Serpens
Aquarius
Pegasus
Pisces
Scorpius
Ophiuchus
Lyra
Cygnus
Milky Way
Hercules
Cepheus
Andromeda
Cetus
Libra
Corona Borealis
Draco
Centaurus
Ursa Minor
Cassiopeia
Aries
Boötes
Perseus
Eridanus
Virgo
Ursa Major
Taurus
Auriga
Leo
Gemini
Cancer
Orion
Hydra
Canis Minor
Canis Major

◄ These seven bright stars in Ursa Major are visible every clear night of the year to Northern-Hemisphere observers. Together they are known as the Big Dipper. The four on the right are the bear's bottom; his tail is marked by the three stars to the left. You may find it easier to picture these stars as a saucepan with the handle on the left.

▲ If you live in the Northern Hemisphere, these are the constellations you can see in the night sky over the course of a year. The dots are the stars. They have been joined together to make constellation patterns. Some, like Leo, are easier to picture than others.

11

The easiest constellation for observers in the Southern Hemisphere to spot is Crux (the Southern Cross). It is the smallest of all the constellations. Close by is Centaurus (the Centaur – a mythical creature, half man and half horse). Centaurus contains both Rigil Kentaurus, the fourth brightest star in the sky, and Proxima Centauri, the closest star to us after the Sun. It is nearly 26 million million miles away. In space, this is quite close. All but 50 stars are over 90 million million miles away.

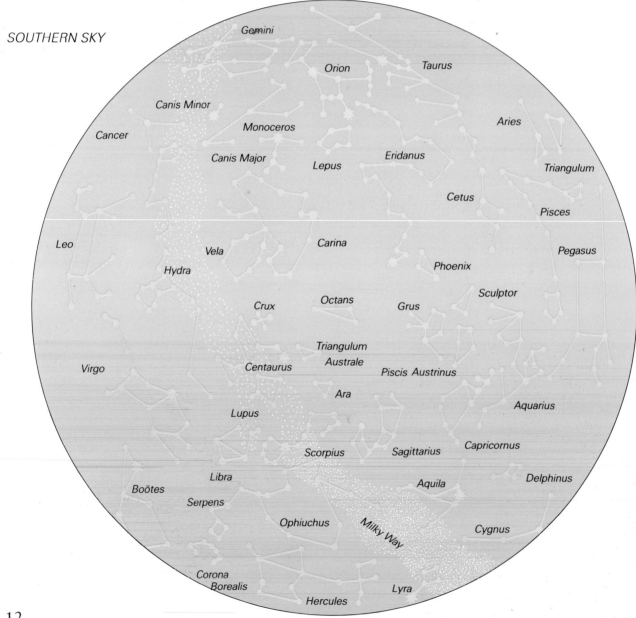

SOUTHERN SKY

► The smallest constellation of all, Crux, is near the center of this southern-sky picture. It may be small, but it is easy to see. Its brilliant cross of stars stands out against the background of the Milky Way. The two bright stars at the top left of this view are in the constellation Centaurus. The one on the left is Rigil Kentaurus, the fourth brightest star in the sky.

◄ The constellations of the southern sky. The ones in the center can be seen all year round. Those nearer the edge are only seen at certain times of the year. Use easily identified constellations like Crux as a starting point to explore the rest of the sky.

If you compare the two star maps, you will soon find that some constellations are on both. These constellations can be seen from both hemispheres, as long as you are not too close to the North Pole or the South Pole. Look out for Taurus, Orion, and Canis Major (the Great Dog), which includes Sirius (the Dog Star), the second brightest star. Leo, Scorpius, and Sagittarius (the Archer) also have very clear star patterns. But you must remember that the time and date when you are observing affect what you can see.

Some constellations are always in the sky. Others rise and set like the Sun. The height they reach in the sky also changes, just as the Sun's does. So during part of the year these stars are high enough to be seen, but at other times you can't see them. Orion is one of the easiest constellations to spot in the evening sky during January and February, then Leo takes over in April and May. The Summer Triangle, which links bright stars in three constellations, appears in August and September. Then Pegasus is seen in November and December.

Wandering stars

Part of the fascination of the night sky is that things are not always what they seem. You can amaze your friends by pointing to a bright light that looks like a star, and telling them it is a planet. But how do you know the difference?

At first glance, planets look like stars. Look again, and you'll notice that a planet is not a pinpoint of light but has some shape to it. It is a circle of light. You can see the difference more clearly through binoculars. The name *planet*, which comes from the Greek word for "wanderer," gives us another clue. Planets follow different paths from the stars. All the stars appear to move together, so if there is one that moves differently from the rest, it could be a planet. But don't expect to see the stars or planets move as you watch them. You'll need to observe them over the course of an evening, or for a number of evenings, to see them move across the sky.

Your friends will be even more amazed if you can tell them which planet it is you can see. Earth and eight other planets all travel around the Sun. The two planets closest to the Sun are Mercury and Venus. Next comes Earth, then Mars, Jupiter, Saturn, Uranus, Neptune, and Pluto.

Mercury is so close to the Sun, and Uranus, Neptune, and Pluto so far away, that they are difficult to see. If you see a planet, it is likely to be Venus, Mars, Jupiter, or Saturn. The brightest and easiest to see is Venus. It is sometimes called the morning or evening star. Look for it in the east just before morning light, or in the west as it starts to get dark.

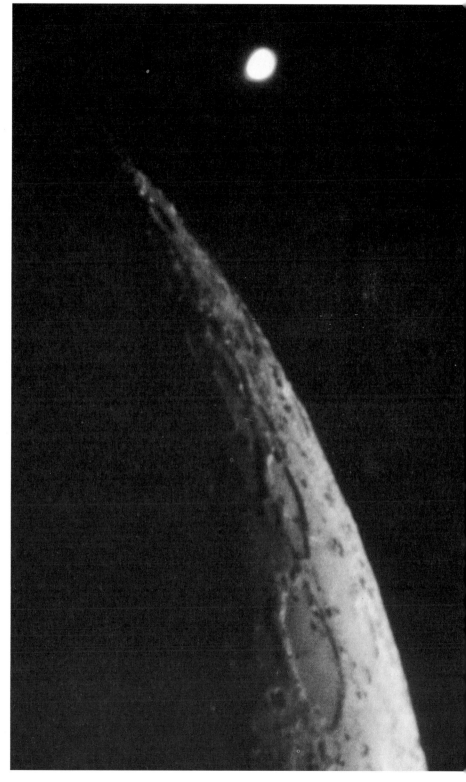

◀ There are two planets in this February sky. Saturn is the top of the three bright ''stars'' in the center of the picture. Mars is in the middle. The lower one is a star in the constellation of Libra.

▶ The planets do not have any light of their own, but reflect light from the Sun. Venus (*top*) does not always receive light on the whole of its surface and so it has phases like our Moon (*left*).

Distant worlds

Jupiter is the largest of all the planets in the solar system. This enormous ball of gas is larger than all the other planets put together. It shines brightly in the night sky for most of the year, moving slowly against the background of stars. Although Jupiter is around 390 million miles from Earth, we can see some of its details. Through a telescope, it looks like a yellowish disk with some darker streaks across it. These are bands of swirling gas which change appearance as the gas clouds move around. Among them is the Great Red Spot, an area of circling gas. This spot and four of Jupiter's 16 known moons – Io, Europa, Ganymede, and Callisto – have been observed by astronomers for over 300 years.

Astronomers have learned a great deal more about the planets from recent visits by space probes. The beautiful planet of Saturn, which is also made largely of gas, has over 20 moons and a series of rings surrounding it. Photographs taken from Voyager space probes showed us that the rings are made of millions of tiny pieces of ice-coated rock.

The Voyager probes also visited the distant worlds of Uranus and Neptune. Both these planets look like greenish-blue disks, but Neptune has some dark bands and several dark spots. Astronomers have only known about Uranus since 1781 and about Neptune since 1846. Most recently discovered was Pluto, which was first seen in 1930. Astronomers don't expect to find any more planets in our solar system.

▶ Jupiter seen through a telescope from Earth. You can see two dark bands of gas clouds across the planet's center, as well as two moons nearby. The moons are two of the four Galilean moons – Io, Europa, Ganymede, and Callisto – which were discovered by Galileo in 1610, using the recently invented telescope. Regular observers of the moons will see them circle around Jupiter.

▲ The Voyager space probes provided our best information yet on the outer planets. Here is beautiful Saturn and six of its largest moons.

► Neptune was the last planet to be visited by Voyager 2, in August 1989. It is a very cold, dim world. Neptune and its eight moons are thirty times further from the Sun and receive 900 times less heat than the Earth.

Star families

Many of the stars in the sky have a twin. The two stars, known as binary or double stars, circle around each other. To the naked eye they often look like a single star, but sometimes binoculars or a telescope will reveal that they are a pair.

Other stars are grouped together into clusters. There may be a few hundred or a few thousand stars in each cluster.

The brightest cluster in the whole sky is the Pleiades, in the constellation of Taurus. It contains stars that are quite young – only about 50 million years old. You can see six or seven of the stars with your eyes, but binoculars will show many more and telescopes can show three to four hundred stars.

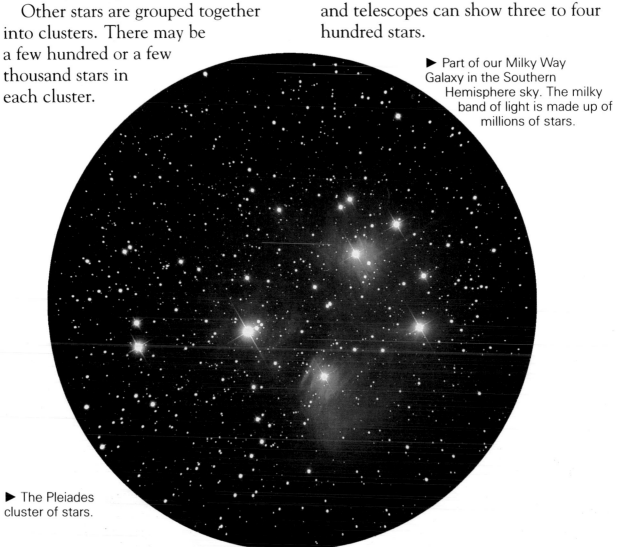

▶ Part of our Milky Way Galaxy in the Southern Hemisphere sky. The milky band of light is made up of millions of stars.

▶ The Pleiades cluster of stars.

In the Southern Hemisphere, the constellation of Crux includes the Jewel Box cluster. It was given its name by the astronomer John Herschel, who thought its stars looked like multicolored jewels.

Galaxies are groupings of very large numbers of stars. The Sun and the stars scattered across our night sky belong to the Milky Way Galaxy. It contains 100,000 million stars. If you look toward the large constellation of Sagittarius, you are looking toward the heart of our Galaxy. The stars look rather like a hazy river of milky light stretching across the sky. This is why they are called the Milky Way.

Other galaxies are so far away they look like fuzzy patches of light in the night sky. The Andromeda Galaxy, nearly 13 million million million miles from Earth, is the most distant object visible to the naked eye.

The Moon

The Moon is the Earth's companion in space, and they journey around the Sun together. Although the Moon has no light of its own, it is the brightest object in the night sky. It simply reflects sunlight.

As the Moon travels around the Earth, our view of it is always changing. Sometimes we see its full face, at other times only its crescent-shaped edge. When the Moon is exactly between the Earth and the Sun, the side facing us has no light on it, so we cannot see it. We call this the *new moon*. There are 29½ days from one new moon to the next. During this lunar month we see all the different shapes, or phases, of the Moon.

By using only your eyes, you can see some of the Moon's surface features. Easily seen are dark, flat areas of land. These are called *maria*, from the Latin *mare*, meaning sea, because early astronomers thought they were seas. The lighter areas are mountains.

Using binoculars, you can see some of the craters that cover a large part of the Moon's surface. Some scientists think these steep-sided hollows were formed when the Moon was bombarded by meteorites – rocks hurtling through space at tens of thousands of miles per hour. Most of this happened when the Moon was young, about 4,000 million years ago. Because there is no water or air on the Moon, its surface has changed very little since then.

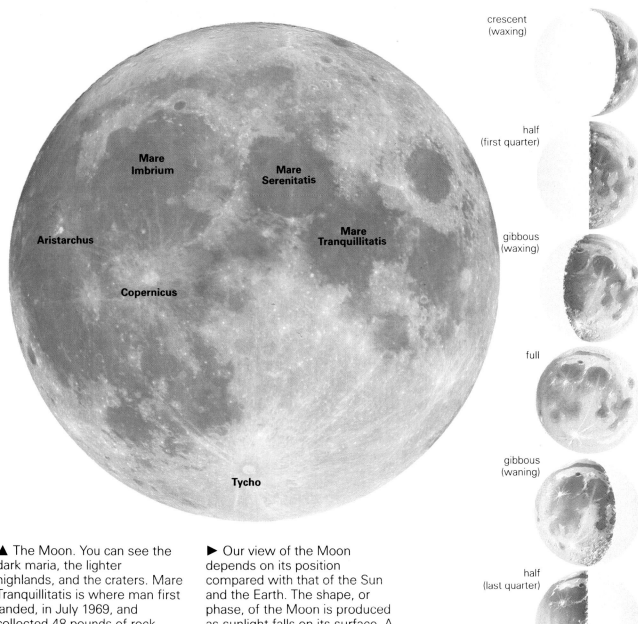

Mare Imbrium

Mare Serenitatis

Aristarchus

Mare Tranquillitatis

Copernicus

Tycho

crescent (waxing)

half (first quarter)

gibbous (waxing)

full

gibbous (waning)

half (last quarter)

crescent (waning)

▲ The Moon. You can see the dark maria, the lighter highlands, and the craters. Mare Tranquillitatis is where man first landed, in July 1969, and collected 48 pounds of rock. Crater Aristarchus is the brightest point on the Moon's surface.

◄ The boundary between the sunlit and the dark areas of the Moon is called the terminator. Craters are most easily viewed near this line.

► Our view of the Moon depends on its position compared with that of the Sun and the Earth. The shape, or phase, of the Moon is produced as sunlight falls on its surface. A lunar month, which lasts 29½ days, is the time it takes for the Moon to go through a complete cycle.

Eclipses

The Moon can look particularly spectacular when it is in eclipse. This happens when the Earth is between the Sun and the Moon. The Moon is then in the Earth's shadow, so it receives almost no light from the Sun. It can take several hours for the Moon to move completely out of the shadow. There are usually two or three lunar eclipses (eclipses of the Moon) every year. If you have a chance to see one, it is well worth watching.

A solar eclipse (an eclipse of the Sun) can only be seen from certain areas on Earth. During a solar eclipse, it is the Moon that is between the Sun and the Earth. The Moon's disk covers the Sun's disk, and stops sunlight from reaching Earth. As the Moon moves in front of the Sun, the Moon casts a shadow, called the *umbra*, which moves across the Earth. If you are in the path of the umbra, you will witness a total eclipse, with the Sun completely covered by the Moon.

▼ The Moon in total eclipse. The Earth is stopping sunlight from reaching the Moon's surface.

At either side of the umbra is an area of lesser shadow, called the *penumbra*. These areas will experience a partial eclipse, with the Sun only partly covered up.

A total eclipse lasts only a few minutes. Day suddenly turns to night as the Sun's light is blocked out. We know why this happens, but ancient people didn't. They were terrified. To them, it seemed as if the world was coming to an end. Some thought a dragon was trying to eat the Sun, and so they banged gongs to scare it away.

▲ During a solar eclipse, the disk of the Sun is hidden behind the Moon. But we can see its outer gases, called its *corona*.

▼ When a solar eclipse is about to start, or end, a bright flash of sunlight appears.

Comets and meteors

Comets and meteors are wonderful to watch, but you won't see them every night. Comets are snowballs of ice and dust, but much, much larger than any snowball you might make. In fact, Halley's Comet, last seen in our skies in 1986, is about 10 miles long and 5 miles wide. It travels in an *orbit*, or path, around the Sun, journeying from the very edge of our solar system.

Close to the Sun, it develops tails of gas and dust which reflect sunlight. These tails can be hundreds of thousands of miles in length and are visible from Earth.

Halley's Comet takes about 76 years to complete its journey. The next time we can see it will be in 2061. Encke's Comet and some others visit our skies more often. But most comets travel such enormous distances that we only see them every few hundred or thousand years.

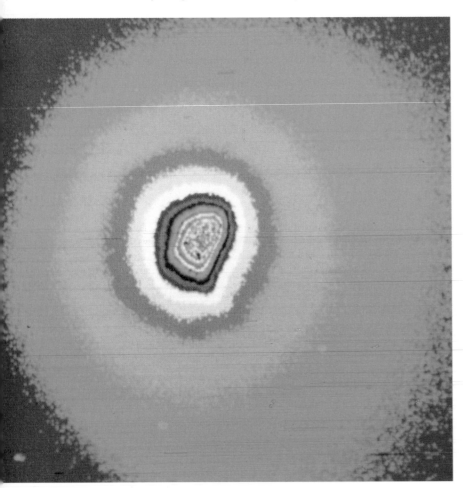

▶ This photograph of Halley's Comet was taken from Australia on March 13, 1986. On this same day a European spacecraft, called Giotto, was making its closest approach to the comet. Giotto took images of the comet's head, or nucleus. Meanwhile, astronomers on Earth photographed the comet from much further away, and their views showed the broad, white dust tail, and the thin, blue gas tail (*right*).

◀ Astronomers use computers to help them in their work. Computers make mathematical calculations much faster than the human brain, and they can also enhance images of astronomical objects. This image of Halley's Comet was made by astronomers using the biggest telescope in the Southern Hemisphere. They then used powerful computers to bring out details in the image. Color has been used to show the different light levels of the comet.

As comets travel along their orbits, they lose some of their dust. When dust from a comet, or a particle of rock, enters the Earth's atmosphere, it burns up. We see it as a streak of light flashing across the sky. This is a meteor. Sometimes meteors are called shooting stars, because they look like stars falling from the sky.

On certain nights throughout the year, you can see meteor showers. Lots of particles appear as bright lights raining down from one particular area of the sky. Look for the Orionid shower around October 21st. It is made up of particles from Halley's Comet.

Taking a look

There are some marvelous sights in the night sky. With a little patience and some good clear skies, you'll soon be familiar with them.

If you have difficulty remembering the constellations, you may find it helps to make your own pictures. Place some tracing paper over one of the star maps in the book. Trace the dots which represent the stars, but don't trace the lines. Then connect the dots to make your own pictures. You may find that Orion looks more like a robot than a hunter, and Crux looks like a kite rather than a cross.

At first, all the stars look silvery-white. But after a few nights of observing, you will notice that some have a very faint coloring. The color comes from the temperature of the star's surface. The hottest stars are blue, and slightly cooler ones are white. Stars that are cooler still are yellow, and the coolest are red.

There is no need to buy expensive equipment to look at the sky. You can see hundreds of objects just by using your eyes. But, if you have the chance, borrow some binoculars. They are easy to use and show as much as a small telescope. They'll reveal thousands more stars, as well as details on the Moon's surface. If you are eager to make a more detailed study of the sky, why not join your local astronomical society? They'll give you helpful advice and information, and may even have a large telescope you can look through.

▶ It's fun to stargaze with friends or family. If you want to share your interest with even more people, then join your local astronomical society. They'll also have up-to-date information on what is happening in the sky.

► The stars in the constellation of Orion are all quite different. Astronomers can calculate a star's age and the different chemicals it is made of, as well as its temperature. You can see a difference in the stars by just using your eyes. Look at the two stars in the shoulders of Orion. The one on the right is a red star, the one on the left is a blue star. These colors indicate how hot the stars are.

▼ Astronomers make accurate records of their observations, drawing as well as writing about what they see. Start a diary and sketch-book of your observations. Note down what you saw and the time you saw it. Compare what something looks like from one night to the next. Draw the shape of the Moon as it changes through the lunar month. Or borrow some binoculars to see how they can change a view. Try counting the new stars you can see with the help of the binoculars. You'll find it easier if you support the binoculars to stop them from wobbling around.

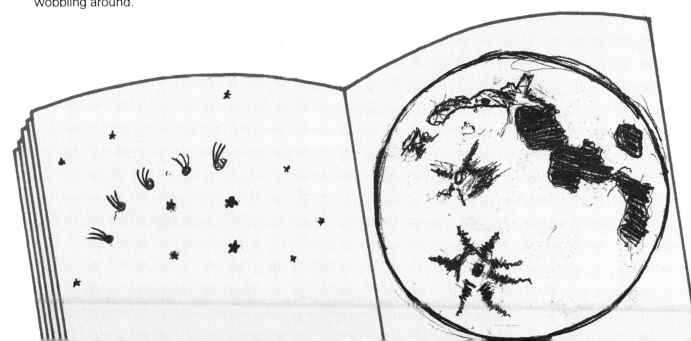

Observatories and telescopes

To take a really detailed look at the sky, astronomers use very large, specially designed telescopes. These have a mirror or a lens to collect the light from an object. The light then passes down the telescope to equipment that records the view. The astronomer controls the telescope with a computer, and a screen (like a television screen) shows what is being recorded. At the end of the observing session, the astronomer can take the records away and study them whenever he or she wants to.

The best observatories usually have two or three big telescopes with mirrors or lenses 3 feet or more across. They are protected inside buildings with domed roofs until they are needed. The domes are opened and the telescopes are pointed to the area of the sky the astronomers want to study.

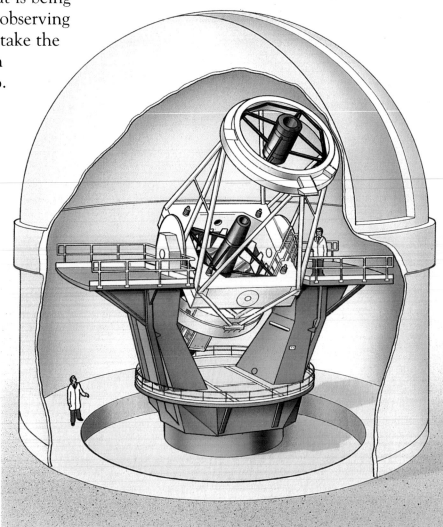

▶ This is one of the world's finest telescopes. It is on the Canary Island of La Palma. The computer-driven mounting supports the telescope and enables it to follow an object across the sky. The most important part of the telescope is its circular mirror, which is over 13 feet across. It is situated at one end of the telescope tube, seen here between the two arms of the mount. The mirror collects the light from an object in the sky, and then directs it to recording equipment attached to the telescope. The tube of the telescope is a skeleton framework, to make it as light as possible, so that the telescope is easy to use.

Many of the world's observatories are built on top of high mountains, so astronomers can observe in the clear sky above the clouds. They are also a long way from cities, since city lights make the sky too bright to see faint stars and galaxies. Some observatories have small hotels as well as offices, workshops, and even an airfield so that astronomers can travel easily to and from the observatory.

But binoculars at home and telescopes in observatories are not the only ways of observing the stars and planets. Astronomers also use satellites and space probes to carry observing and recording equipment into space. By observing the sky and exploring space, we are learning more about our universe all the time.

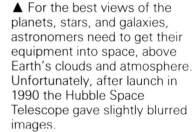

▲ For the best views of the planets, stars, and galaxies, astronomers need to get their equipment into space, above Earth's clouds and atmosphere. Unfortunately, after launch in 1990 the Hubble Space Telescope gave slightly blurred images.

◄ The best observatories on Earth are on mountain tops, well away from cities, giving clear views of the sky above. This means they are very expensive to build. Countries join together to share the costs. This is the European Southern Observatory in Chile, South America. It houses 14 large telescopes.

Fact file

Starry sky

There are almost six thousand stars visible to the naked eye. But they are not all visible at one time. If you are viewing stars from a city, only two or three hundred at most may be seen. The number rises to about forty-three thousand if you use a pair of binoculars.

A closer look

People used only their eyes to look at the heavens until the early 1600s, when the telescope was invented. Today, astronomers send their telescopes into space aboard satellites and spacecraft to get the best views possible. The Hubble Space Telescope, launched in April 1990, is intended to pick up light from objects fifty times fainter than any telescope on Earth.

The search for life

When two spacecraft touched down on Mars in 1976, one of their jobs was to look for signs of life. They used a 10-foot robot arm to collect and analyze rock samples, but no life-supporting material was found. Earth is still the only planet known to have life.

▶ Viking 1 collecting rock samples on Mars.

The dark side of the Moon

The same face of the Moon is turned earthward all the time. The first views of the far side of the Moon were obtained by spacecraft in 1959.

Lunar craters

The brightest crater on the Moon is Aristarchus. The craters Tycho and Copernicus are also easy to see. You can locate all of these on the photograph on page 21.

Solar eclipse

There are usually two, and occasionally three, solar eclipses each year. The longest time a total eclipse can last is 7 minutes and 31 seconds. But astronomers have managed to observe an eclipse for longer than this by being aboard a Concorde aircraft flying in the Moon's shadow and keeping pace with it as it passed across the Earth.

Constellation facts

The sky is divided into 88 constellations. The largest is Hydra, the Water Snake, and the smallest is Crux, the Southern Cross.

The zodiac

The system of constellations along the Sun's yearly path is called the zodiac. The planets and the Moon also move within the band of sky marked by these stars. The term "zodiac" comes from the Greek for animal. The zodiac is a circle of animals and people, with one exception, Libra. The zodiac constellations are:

Aries	The Ram
Taurus	The Bull
Gemini	The Twins
Cancer	The Crab
Leo	The Lion
Virgo	The Virgin
Libra	The Scales
Scorpius	The Scorpion
Sagittarius	The Archer
Capricornus	The Sea Goat
Aquarius	The Water Carrier
Pisces	The Fishes

Star names

Many bright stars in the sky have their own names. Over two hundred of the star names in common use come from the Arabic language. One example is Betelgeuse, the bright star in Orion. Betelgeuse comes from a poor translation of the original Arabic meaning "the hand of Orion." The star actually marks one of Orion's shoulders.

Star brightness

Astronomers use two scales of numbers to indicate how bright a star is. The *absolute magnitude* scale refers to a star's real brightness. As a stargazer, you'll want to know the *apparent magnitude* of a star, its brightness as seen from Earth. The bigger the number a star is given, the fainter the star. The faintest stars detected with Earth-based telescopes are magnitude 24. Stars brighter than magnitude 1 are given a zero or negative rating. Most people can see stars as faint as magnitude 4. Binoculars will show stars to magnitude 8. The apparent magnitudes of the six brightest stars in the sky are:

Sun	−26.70
Sirius	−1.46
Canopus	−0.72
Rigil Kentaurus	−0.27
Arcturus	−0.04
Vega	0.03

Star distance

Distances across space are so vast that the Earth-based measuring system using miles is just not manageable. The numbers needed to identify such long distances are too big and unwieldy to use. That's why astronomers use light-years to measure distance in space. Light travels 5.88 million million miles in one year. The bright star Sirius is 8.8 light-years away from us. Or, put another way, the light we receive from Sirius left that star 8.8 years ago. The closest star to us is, of course, the Sun, only 8.3 light-minutes away. Only fifty stars are closer than 16 light-years, and most are much, much farther away. The most distant object you can see with the naked eye is the Andromeda Galaxy, 2.2 million light-years away.

▼ Sirius (at the bottom of the picture) is the brightest star in the night sky.

▲ The Large Magellanic Cloud, a nearby irregular galaxy.

The Local Group

Our Milky Way Galaxy belongs to a group of around thirty galaxies called the Local Group. The largest galaxy in the group is the Andromeda Galaxy. It is around one and a half times the size of our Galaxy. Also in the Local Group are the Triangulum Galaxy and the Large and Small Magellanic Clouds.

Index